ARCHITECTURE & DESIGN LIBRARY

ARTS AND CRAFTS

ARTS AND CRAFTS

Kitty Turgeon and Robert Rust

FRIEDMAN/FAIRFAX

PUBLISHERS

A FRIEDMAN/FAIRFAX BOOK

© 1997 by Michael Friedman Publishing Group, Inc.

Library of Congress Cataloging-in-Publication data

Rust, Robert
    Arts & crafts / Robert Rust and Kitty Turgeon.
        p. cm. -- (Architecture and design library : 4)
    Includes index.
    ISBN 1-56799-363-X (hc)
    1. Arts and crafts movement--England.   2. Arts and crafts
movement--United States.   I. Turgeon, Kitty.   II. Title.
III. Series.
NK 1142.R87   1997
745'.0942--dc20   96-28958

Editor: Susan Lauzau
Art Director: Lynne Yeamans
Layout: Robbi O. Firestone
Photography Editor: Wendy Missan
Production Manager: Camille Lee

Color separations by Bright Arts Graphics (S) Pte Ltd.
Printed in Hong Kong by Midas Printing Limited

For bulk purchases and special sales, please contact:
Friedman/Fairfax Publishers
Attention: Sales Department
15 West 26th Street
New York, New York 10010
212/685-6610   FAX 212/685-1307

Visit our website:
http://www.metrobooks.com

To the Roycroft Renaissance and to Alexis Jean Fournier,
whose house we love and live in

Contents

INTRODUCTION

"Have nothing in your home that is not functional or that you do not believe to be beautiful."

—William Morris

The Arts and Crafts Movement is in full revival in the 1990s, and it is now—just as it was at the turn of the nineteenth century—a philosophy as well as a style. Arts and Crafts means more than bungalows, Mission style, and Craftsman pieces, though it encompasses all of these. To truly understand the Arts and Crafts style, we must first look at the beliefs and values that shaped the movement.

The Arts and Crafts Movement began in 1860s England with the ideas of philosopher John Ruskin and designer and poet William Morris. These influential thinkers idealized medieval times, and held that society would benefit from a return to an economic system in which workers were valued and natural materials and painstaking handiwork were highly regarded. During the Middle Ages, craftsmen were held in esteem and the guild system monitored their efforts, ensuring high standards for all goods. Pride of workmanship and a sense of accomplishment were social benefits that would come with fine design and well-made goods.

But not all of the exponents of the British Arts and Crafts Movement rejected the machine in favor of handcrafting. A notable exception was the Englishman Christopher Dresser, who believed that it was the way machines were used that was misguided; he favored instead a reinvention of machines and processes to emphasize quality designs and products. Even William Morris, considered the father of the Arts and Craft Movement, thought that drudgery could be eliminated with machines, provided that the rest of the work was done with care by hand.

A middle-class society made happy and whole by a return to the basic, simple styles of the past never really materialized. In England, only the wealthy could afford the beautiful, lovingly crafted pieces. What persevered instead was the idea that people could achieve dignity,

OPPOSITE: *This inspiring leaded-glass window at the Roycroft Inn was designed around 1908 by Roycrofter Dard Hunter, who is perhaps best known as a graphic artist and paper maker. The pointed arch is a feature of the Gothic era that the Arts and Crafts designers so admired, while the stylized tulip reflects their fascination with the natural world.*

respectability, and refinement by surrounding themselves with furnishings of quality and style.

The Arts and Crafts Movement found its own expression in North America from about 1890 to 1920, evolving into a style distinct from its British counterpart. Elbert Hubbard and Gustav Stickley, American visitors to England, listened to the philosophy behind the Arts and Crafts lifestyle and came back to New York State to put the theories into practice at the Roycroft Shops in East Aurora and United Crafts in Syracuse, respectively. Artisans at these communities, and other American Arts and Crafts designers as well, embraced the machine rather than abandoning it, giving the Arts and Crafts Movement in North America a different twist.

In North America, furnishings of good design and quality workmanship became a reality—at least at the upper-middle-class level. The new attitudes toward nature and its healing properties were detailed in several Arts and Crafts magazines. *The Craftsman* was published by Stickley; two Roycroft periodicals, *The Philistine* and *The Fra*, took the message to subscribers, while Hubbard went on the lecture circuit.

The reverence for nature inherent in Arts and Crafts philosophy soon gave birth to the environmental movement. The creation of national parks became a priority, and the National Geographic Society and the Sierra Club were born. "Wilderness escapes" became the thing to do. As part of this movement back to the land and to simpler times, Native American primitive designs (rugs, pottery, jewelry, and baskets) were preserved and vacation homes in the style of lodges, cabins, and seaside bungalows became popular.

Physical culture, good nutrition, and personal responsibility for one's own health were advocated. The wise marched off to the seashore, lakeside, mountains, or countryside for healthful vacations, and some even stayed there. California, especially, drew those who were interested in these new attitudes, and consequently there are more bungalows in California than anywhere else.

At the same time, the three-hundred-year-old Spanish missions that dotted California and the Southwest gave these new pilgrims inspiration, and preserving these historic buildings became part of their agenda. The term "Mission" became associated with the style, a subset of Arts and Crafts, that grew out of admiration for the old Spanish buildings and their furnishings.

On the way west the Arts and Crafts style left its mark in the Midwest as well. Called Prairie to match the landscape, the Arts and Crafts style was adapted by regional designers, who established their own societies and varied the architecture and furnishings to suit their surroundings.

The Arts and Crafts ideal fit the American ethic of work, health, wealth, and individuality so well that it became *the* style. Not only did the philosophy influence social behavior, it revolutionized architecture and interior design as well. Each region had its own vernacular expression; buildings were seen to be part of the environment, and the use of natural materials was an integral part of the movement.

Arts and Crafts style as interior design depends on simplicity and harmony among the home's many elements. The lifestyle it advocates is holistic and planet-friendly, an attitude even more appealing in the 1990s than it was a hundred years ago. In the last third of the twentieth century, the Arts and Crafts renaissance has emerged as a sophisticated alternative to more modern designs, in which the importance of the individual in the creation of his home is often ignored. Arts and Crafts enthusiasts are growing in number, attracted by the style's comfortable emphasis on quality, communication, and family values.

An appreciation for Arts and Crafts–era history helps us redefine the look in a more sophisticated way for today. Called a backlash to the Industrial Revolution, the original Arts and Crafts Movement was a reaction to technological progress, a refocusing on creations of the heart and hand. As we explore Arts and Crafts interiors, it is clear that the style is not a new fad, but rather a trend becoming a classic.

RIGHT: *A reissued Roycroft cabinet displays a collection of Arts and Crafts objects and a plein air painting. The hardware was inspired by medieval designs, and reinforces the Arts and Crafts urge to create a nineteenth-century Camelot. In quartersawn oak with canted sides, the piece looks lovely against the rich mottled yellow of the walls.*

LEFT: *Indoor bathrooms were a new addition to houses in the Arts and Crafts era, and their decor was generally quite simple. Gleaming tile, porcelain, and white paint are the traditional outfittings of the Arts and Crafts bath.*

RIGHT: *Sideboards and plate rails make ideal surfaces for displaying collections of art pottery and metal. Nature is once again the source of inspiration for the decorative details in the room—a bowl of green apples, an arrangement of hot-colored flowers, a plein air painting above the buffet, and an embroidered center cloth on the table all testify to the place that nature holds in Arts and Crafts decorating.*

ABOVE: *These plastered exterior walls with generous overhangs and wood trim are typical of houses in the Prairie style, the foremost Arts and Crafts architecture in the Midwest. Prairie style emphasizes horizontal lines that blend in with the flat planes of the surrounding landscape.*

RIGHT: *The natural look of this restored sleeping porch is achieved with beadboard walls and ceiling. Expanses of wood are softened by rich red William Morris wallpaper and a broadloom carpet reminiscent of an old-fashioned rag rug. A wicker chair, roll-down blinds, and white bed linens contribute to the authenticity of this original "healthy" bedchamber.*

CHAPTER ONE

EXTERIORS

An Arts and Crafts house, by definition, fits into the landscape surrounding it as if it were meant to be there. The house must not only complement, but make good use of, its surroundings—the use of indigenous construction materials celebrates each geographical region. This adaptation of architectural styles to suit the building's location—a hallmark of the Arts and Crafts style—resulted in Craftsman houses with diverse exterior facades and many different types of building stock.

Arts and Crafts houses are often identified as such by their interior similarities, since their exteriors show vast differences in style. In fact, quality construction and compatibility with the surrounding countryside are the only guidelines in labeling a house as Arts and Crafts style.

The Arts and Crafts houses of various regions share certain traits, however. The homes in New England most clearly reveal the British roots of the style. English Tudor houses made of stone or brick with half-timbered beams and rough stucco grace the landscape. These examples are handsome and somewhat formal, regardless of their size.

Wooded mountain and lake areas in both the eastern and western parts of North America are ideal sites for log cabins, whether the one-room variety, the elegant summer camps built by turn-of-the-century railroad magnates and wealthy oil barons, or the lodges built in state and national parks.

ABOVE: *Mottoes carved into doors and window frames, both indoors and out, are a common Arts and Crafts feature. This beautiful door welcomes guests to the historic Roycroft Inn.*

OPPOSITE: *Craftsman Farms, Gustav Stickley's home in Parsippany, New Jersey, is one of the most famous Arts and Crafts log houses. The massive stone chimneys, log construction, and tile roof give this landmark a distinctively American look, while leaded diamond windows are a nod to the movement's English heritage.*

The term "Craftsman house" is familiar when referring to the one-and-a-half- to two-story houses built outside cities before and after World War I. While only the houses designed for Gustav Stickley's *Craftsman* magazine are truly Craftsman homes, the designation has come into generic use and many cozy cottages are called Craftsman style.

The Midwest is the setting for horizontal Prairie houses that were designed to blend into the landscape. These houses are generally made of brick or stucco, or a combination of both. Frank Lloyd Wright's early designs offer many excellent examples of this style.

In the South and West, unique bungalows dot the coastal landscape. The original definition of "bungalow" came from India and referred to one-story houses with long, steep, overhanging rooflines that were built to protect British colonists from the heat and harsh sun. The bungalow soon became synonymous with the good life in the deliciously warm climates of Florida and California.

Imitating the Spanish missions and Native American pueblos of coastal California and New Mexico, a style of stucco-covered houses with thick, pale peach or whitewashed walls and tiled roofs became popular in the West. This style was also well suited to government buildings and hotels, and many early-twentieth-century structures reflect the mission influence.

Even the boxy, four-square houses that traditionally represent the middle class can be classified as Arts and Crafts homes if their interiors include the typical finishes, built-ins, and fireplaces.

The sleeping porch was another feature that bridged the gap between interior and exterior. Sleeping in the fresh air in a covered or screened outdoor room was the ultimate step toward communing with nature and improving one's health.

One requirement of all Arts and Crafts homes is a garden; even urban Arts and Crafts row houses include a small bed of flowers and vegetables. The garden as a source of nourishment for the body and soul is still a vital part of the Arts and Crafts lifestyle. Porches, window boxes, and pergolas provide links between the house and garden. Traditional plantings for Arts and Crafts gardens are derived mainly from English cottage gardens, which brim with informally arranged perennial flowers, herbs, and vegetables. As in all other elements of the Arts and Crafts Movement, the garden style was in direct contrast to the contrived, overly formal Victorian style.

ABOVE: *The courtyard garden of the landmark Roycroft Inn uses the fireplace chimney as a focal point. The original peristyle (a columned covered walkway) has been restored, and now stands as it was in 1905 when the inn was built. The peristyle was also a typical feature in several Frank Lloyd Wright buildings of the period.*

OPPOSITE: *This traditional one-story bungalow is complete with a wraparound porch. The heavy brick porch supports give this small house an aura of substance, while airy white posts and railings and wide steps prevent the front from appearing too solid.*

LEFT: *This California clinker brick garden wall is inset with Arts and Crafts tiles cast by the potter Ernest Batchelder, who favored designs derived from medieval and Oriental motifs. Clinker brick was brick originally rejected after the firing process because of irregularities in the brick's shape or surface. It became a favorite material of Arts and Crafts architects for the earthy, more natural look it contributed.*

RIGHT: *The porch is of paramount importance in the Arts and Crafts house and lifestyle. Used for alfresco dining, reading, relaxing, and entertaining, this porch adds elegant space with its slate floor, sturdy yet comfortable furniture, and Craftsman-style lanterns. Bringing plants onto the porch provides visual links between the area and the garden beyond.*

ABOVE: *This large native stone and cedar shake-shingled ranch-style house in Flagstaff, Arizona, features a pergola on either side of the front entrance, though only one of the pergolas is visible from this angle. This architectural element is a charming transition from the out-of-doors to interior space.*

ABOVE: *The Fournier House, a Tudor-style two-story in East Aurora, New York, has been painted in period Arts and Crafts colors. The combination of weathered shingle siding, dark bottle green trim, and bird's-eye maple–colored detailing is designed to highlight the house's architectural details, such as corbels, columns, and timber structure.*

LEFT: *English Tudor architecture is one of the hallmarks of the British Arts and Crafts Movement; the style is prevalent throughout England and on the East Coast of North America as well. This half-timbered upper story sits solidly on a first floor constructed of local stone and red brick.*

RIGHT: *Clinker brick and native boulder construction, along with a subtle blue-green stained trim, distinguish the entrance to the shingle-style Duncan-Irwin House in California. A leaded- and stained-glass door, tiled terrace, Japanese lantern, and high-back corner bench make a grand Arts and Crafts combination for this special house.*

LEFT: *Deep overhanging eaves on a second-floor gallery create a dramatic space that offers both covered porch and open-air balcony. The Prairie-style stained-glass windows add further glamour to this Frank Lloyd Wright house.*

BELOW: *The horizontal Roman brick of this house's facade is a signature feature in the famous Prairie-style Dana-Thomas House, designed by Frank Lloyd Wright. The leaded glass in the long windows (which also appears in other wings of the house) is another special element of the architect-designed houses of the Midwest.*

ABOVE: *Bungalow courts provided inexpensive housing after World War I in sunny California. The spacious circular yard—complete with its surrounding beds of native plants—is shared by all the houses that border the court, offering a spacious garden in an area where square footage is at a premium.*

ABOVE: *Revival-style Spanish Mission stucco appears predominantly in the Southwest. The pleasing arches of the veranda continue in the windows of the living room, bestowing a sense of unity to the house's facade and bridging the gap between interior and exterior spaces.*

LEFT: *Airplane bungalows—named for the attic room reminiscent of a cockpit and for their flared, winglike gables—are found mostly in the West. The two-story section of the house conveniently allows for an extra bedroom or two. The massive piers tie the surrounding wings into the site.*

BELOW: *The long, low overhangs, or eaves, of this Prairie-style house deflect the sun's rays during the hot summer months but allow the low winter sun to illuminate the leaded windows.*

OPPOSITE: *The Gamble House, known as the "ultimate bun-galow," is one of the most fabulous examples of Arts and Crafts bungalows. As is evident from this lavish home, which was de-signed by Greene & Greene, even the wealthy favored Arts and Crafts style.*

ABOVE: *A one-and-a-half-story brick bungalow features a large shed dormer protruding from the roofline. This is classic Arts and Crafts architecture, and is found in every region.*

OPPOSITE: *Mariposa is the name of this Hollywood Hills shingle-style chalet. Like all good Arts and Crafts houses, it is surrounded by a garden in keeping with the native landscape, here a wonderful desert scheme.*

ABOVE: *Natural redwood shingles and Japanesque beveled trim are the only ornamentation required on this California bungalow designed by renowned architects Greene & Greene. Exposed-construction window boxes are typical of these bungalows, and were built into Arts and Crafts houses as effective transitions from outdoors to indoors.*

CHAPTER TWO

INTERIOR DETAILS AND FINISHES

Interior architectural details are an important feature of Arts and Crafts–style houses, and in fact the very definition of a true Arts and Crafts house rests with the interior detailing. Fireplaces, warm-toned woodwork, and built-in bookcases, seating, and sideboards all characterize Craftsman-style interiors.

The fireplace, which serves either as the focal point of a room or as a nostalgic touch, is a must for an Arts and Crafts house. Although the fireplace was not necessarily used for warmth and almost never for cooking (although many were adorned with a crane and pot), it had great symbolic importance in the Arts and Crafts movement. The fireplace stood for security, nourishment, communication, comfort, and, indeed, transformation. Throughout human history, the hearth had provided a gathering space where family and friends could share their troubles and their joys, and the Arts and Crafts philosophy invoked this ancient use of the fireplace. Made of brick or stone, with impressive mantles or copper hoods, the fireplace was the highlight of the new "living room," as well as the centerpiece for that other hallmark of the Craftsman interior: built-ins.

Built-in bookcases on either side of the fireplace (often with leaded-glass windows in the doors or stained-glass windows above them) were standard in even the smallest bungalow. Larger houses

ABOVE: *Hand-hammered copper hardware, signed by Gustav Stickley, is ideally suited to the handmade, substantial look of Arts and Crafts interiors. The doorlatch is affixed to quarter-sawn oak with handsome pyramidal screws.*

OPPOSITE: *The sheen of the hammered-copper hood draws the eye immediately to the massive fireplace, the focal point of this room. Simple benches crowded with colorful pillows create a comfortable sitting area before the fire at Roycroft Shops.*

boasted inglenooks, built-in high-back benches that flanked the fireplace and created snug seating areas. This cozy spot offered a comfortable reason to linger and chat or read, or simply bask in the glow of the fire.

Other built-ins—such as half-walls with a column to the ceiling or two-sided room dividers that might serve as bookcases or display shelves—were often added between the living and dining room. This effectively separated the rooms yet created an open, airy feeling and a sense of intimacy.

Many dining rooms boasted a built-in sideboard above which hung a plain or beveled mirror that reflected a collection of copper, silver, or art pottery. The built-in piece gave the room a sleek look, while the mirror opened up the space and made it appear larger. Sometimes the sideboard extended to a pair of china cabinets. The dining room was most often the room where wood beams highlighted the ceilings, and beautiful paneling extended to chair or plate rail height. The frieze—the area above the plate rail—was an important part of the wall, and was usually decorated with stenciling, wallpaper, murals, or fabric. Since dining as a family was a key to the open communication embraced by the Arts and Crafts lifestyle, the dining room might well be larger than the living room.

An array of smaller details also made the Arts and Crafts interior distinctive. Picture rails were generally attached to walls at ceiling height or just below the frieze. These rails, from which paintings or prints could be hung, ensured that artwork was a part of the Arts and Crafts home, and allowed homeowners to move the pieces about with ease. Window seats were popular features in many rooms of the Arts and Crafts interior, both upstairs and down. Built-in drawers or cupboards, too, are standard elements in Craftsman houses and were built under the steeply sloping eaves in large and small houses alike.

Entrance hallways in Arts and Crafts houses were in direct proportion to the size and importance of the house. The stairway was always open to the foyer and the living area, and the straight-spindled sides of the staircase often formed a railing or a peek-through division that defined the space, making it appear very substantial. More often than not, rich paneling completed the picture.

The division of wall surfaces into three horizontal bands followed William Morris' dictates, and allowed several wall finishes in each room. Paneling topped by a chair rail was used for the wainscot, followed by paper or a different paneling in the middle section and another motif in the frieze.

This wood, paint, and wallpaper treatment was intentionally somewhat dark; the Arts and Crafts interior was meant to be a retreat that re-created nature's earthy tones. The home was viewed as a haven, a respite from the stress of the workaday world.

Bedrooms, however, were designed to be lighter and airier, an attitude more conducive to sweet dreams. There, woodwork was generally painted in pastel shades, and light-colored papers were used.

Today, after off-white and other very light colors have dominated interior design for several decades, we are beginning to again appreciate darker hues, especially in our living and dining rooms. In response to the Arts and Crafts revival, several paint and wallpaper companies have created colors and designs appropriate for Craftsman-style houses.

RIGHT, TOP: *Office furniture has become one of the most popular expressions of the Arts and Crafts style. In this version, a quartersawn oak desk and credenza are designed to look authoritative and functional. Several companies make computer desks and printer tables with a Craftsman/Mission look. A tribal carpet, Prairie-style mullioned window, and earthy green walls complete this serene but formal office.*

RIGHT, BOTTOM: *Arts and Crafts interiors often feature living and dining rooms that are open to each other or separated subtly with French doors. Various Native American patterns on rugs and pillows mix well with basic Craftsman pieces to enliven this cavernous space.*

ABOVE: *The squared arch and accompanying columns divide this music salon from the foyer and dining room beyond. A built-in window seat and bookcase blend into the quartersawn oak paneling in a spacious alcove. Originally, the room boasted murals by Alex Fournier on the frieze; the paintings are now restored.*

LEFT: *The Gamble House living room is a symphony of Arts and Crafts elements: gleaming woodwork, subtle lighting, simple furniture, and distinctive tile are repeated throughout the space. Exposed joinery recalls and celebrates the handiwork of early house builders, with whom Arts and Crafts designers felt a strong affinity.*

LEFT: *Strong ceiling beams, a high wainscot, and wooden floors are balanced by a pale beige frieze, natural linen on the table, and several shaded light fixtures. The stylized design on the wall, along with the wooden blinds, help break up the somber tone.*

OPPOSITE: *The spindled railing that runs up the staircase and along the gallery dominates this two-story space. The heavy chair and geometric rug, while not Arts and Crafts–style, are appropriately strong designs and set off the delicate twig tables, which are traditional Arts and Crafts accent pieces.*

OPPOSITE: *Interior wall divisions and the mullioned, stained-glass sidelight are typical Arts and Crafts interior features. A wainscot that reaches to the plate rail offers texture in the form of beautifully grained dark wood. The picture rail dividing the frieze allows for versatile wall decoration. This is the entry hall of one of the bungalows designed by the famed Greene brothers of California.*

ABOVE: *Magnificent leaded-glass doors grace the entry hall of the renowned Gamble House. Nature is the theme here as well as throughout the house. Note that the sidelights of the main door are functional, opening to allow maximum ventilation for the interior.*

LEFT: *Art glass windows allow a measure of privacy but provide glorious light and a view of the garden. Designed for the seated height, the bottom portion of the window is quite clear. An added attraction of art glass windows: the designs throw delightful shadow points on the floor.*

OPPOSITE: *Though this Frank Lloyd Wright block house was not built until the 1920s, it still shows Arts and Crafts influence. Resembling a Mayan temple, the house was constructed largely from the clay soil found on the site. The designs of dramatic art glass windows echo other primitive shapes found in the room.*

LEFT: *Window seats were favorites of Arts and Crafts architects. Combined with a sofa, as here, the space provides extra seating without cluttering the room. Piled with soft pillows, a window seat makes an inviting spot for a chat with a friend or for an afternoon read. Note the textiles embroidered with stylized floral designs that decorate the sofa.*

RIGHT: *An inglenook is created here with two built-in, high-back benches that form an intimate room within a room beside the fireplace. The fact that the walls of the inglenook don't extended all the way to the ceiling keeps the space open. A tile floor, which serves as an extended hearth, helps to define the inglenook as a space apart.*

OPPOSITE: *Built by the Roycrofters for their premier artist, Alexis Jean Fournier, this house boasts a dining room that is a masterpiece of Arts and Crafts style. The mural, painted by Fournier, is called* Times of the Day. *Typically the dining room was host to a beamed ceiling; the quartersawn oak plate rail, too, is a characteristic feature of Arts and Crafts dining rooms. A large south window with a built-in seat provides an ideal place for plants.*

ABOVE: *The semicircular opening of the stone fireplace echoes beautifully the arch of the niche in which it is set. This dramatic inglenook makes a cozy conversation area within the main room. An additional chair in the style of 1930s Art Moderne repeats the arch one more time.*

LEFT: *A sleeping porch with a spectacular vaulted log ceiling provides an ideal spot for exercise or relaxation. The multitude of windows offers plenty of fresh air and sunshine, necessities for good health according to the advocates of the Arts and Crafts lifestyle.*

VOL. XV. NO. 6

VOL. XXV. No. 1 APRIL, 1909   25 CEN

THE   TSM

THE CRAFTSM

OCTOBER, 1913

THE CRAFTSMAN

"The lyf so short, the craft so long to lerne"

THE DEMOCRACY OF THE CARPENTER: BY BOUCK WHITE.
THE CRAFTSMAN MOVEMENT AND THE NEW
CRAFTSMAN BUILDING: BY GUSTAV STICKLEY.
NUT TREES AS A SOURCE OF FOOD SUPPLY.
NEW ENGLAND'S LESSON IN CIVIC BEAUTY.
PICTURES OF FAMOUS MODERN LITERARY MEN.
THE CRAFTSMAN BUILDING-NEW YORK CITY

CHAPTER THREE
LIGHTING

The Arts and Crafts house had many features that—at the turn of the twentieth century—represented revolutionary ideas and new technology. Electric lighting, introduced to the world at the Pan American Exhibition of 1901, was the most exciting of these innovations.

After the relatively dim light cast by kerosene and gas lamps, the brighter electric lights took some getting used to. Lamp shades provided some diffusing quality and were not only necessary to tone down the brightness, but were wonderful to look at. By today's standards, however, Arts and Crafts lamps are difficult to read by, as their light is much more subtle than the 100-watt bulbs and halogen lamps we've become used to. Adding modern table and floor lamps to an Arts and Crafts setting is perfectly appropriate, and serves to link our own high-tech age with the technology boom of the Arts and Crafts era.

For lighting that has atmosphere and charm, though, Arts and Crafts hanging lanterns and floor and table lamps are an inspired choice. Stained-glass shades—either geometric in design or in the elegant Tiffany style—add wonderful color and romantic lighting. High-quality reproductions are used by all but museums and some very wealthy collectors. Shades made of copper or wood with panels of mica (a mineral layered with shellac) give off a warm and flattering glow. Another lamp shade option is amber blown glass, which has a look similar to the original Steuben and Tiffany tulip-shaped shades. Even heavy parchment, linen, silk, and frosted or pleated glass were used as shades.

The bases of floor and table lamps were works of art themselves. Some were fashioned of quartersawn oak or cherry wood; others were made of art pottery with matte glazes or hand-painted designs. Bases of cast bronze and hand-hammered copper were even more popular than the wood and pottery versions.

Living rooms were usually lit with several lamps, which were placed around the room in varying combinations. The living room might also boast a central ceiling light, which typically hung low, suspended by chains. These central lights often hung over a library table in the living room, and were also popular in the dining room, where they took center stage over the table. Wall sconces were most often

OPPOSITE: *This nature-themed Tiffany shade features a repeating stylized acorn design on its border. The poppy-embroidered tablecloth, with its bevy of bees, extends the nature theme. Note the vintage copies of Gustav Stickley's periodical* The Craftsman, *resting beside the hand-thrown pottery.*

seen in dining rooms and hallways, where perimeter lighting was valued. Sconces matched one another and generally complemented the ceiling light, creating a harmony between lighting elements as well as a fascinating diversity.

ABOVE: *Narrow slits of windows, the same shape as a trio of hanging lanterns, give dramatic light. Heavy curtains regulate the amount of sunlight the room receives and pick up the tones of the amber-colored windowpanes.*

RIGHT: *The guest quarters of this Frank Lloyd Wright house are illuminated by wall sconces and windows both high and low. Hanging portieres under a beamed ceiling divide the sleeping areas, offering privacy and warmth.*

ABOVE: *A built-in sideboard and china cabinet made of chestnut are the focus of this wonderful dining room. The matching chestnut ceiling beams and paneling are enhanced by the rich russet color of the ceiling, softly lit cabinets, and Arts and Crafts–style carpet. The frieze has been painted a lighter tone in the same color family. Original Roycroft china sets the table and fills the side cupboard.*

ABOVE: *A stained-glass lamp with a wooden base is a perfect foil for the spindle chair, trestle table, and Oriental rug in this wonderful workspace. The rich combination is enhanced by the ever-present fireplace, also a source of ambient light in the Arts and Crafts interior.*

ABOVE: *These Craftsman-style hanging light fixtures sport aurene glass shades. Candlelight, too, is suitable for Arts and Crafts dining rooms, and complements the warm glow typical of period lighting. Note that the wainscot, which runs up to the plate rail around most of the room, drops down on the server side. Leather chair seats and the tile floor are in keeping with Arts and Crafts–style ideals, in which easy cleaning was an important virtue.*

OPPOSITE: *Note how the lighting in this room circles the space: a fireplace casts warm light; beside it stands a sunny window; to the right of the window is a tiny Arts and Crafts wall sconce. Further along the wall is a fabulous example of a mica and copper lamp. Rounding out the room, a lamp with a gleaming copper shade rests on a tile-top table. The massive sideboard is Stickley reproduction. The carpet, pottery, flowers, textiles, painting, and lighting give color and definition to the vast expanses of wood. This balance is essential for good Arts and Crafts decorating.*

ABOVE: *Hanging lamps and wall sconces are reminiscent of the simple Japanese lanterns so admired by Arts and Crafts designers. A bamboo window shade effectively controls the amount of light admitted by the large picture window. Floral but not fussy, the carpet lightens the mood of the wide-slatted Mission furniture. This is the room of someone very much in touch with nature.*

OPPOSITE: *The billiard room of this lavish but rustic mountain camp is lit with both direct and indirect light, highlighting the room's airy construction. Frosted glass globes screwed into rough-hewn beams are suspended from the ceiling with chains, and are complemented by wall lamps of the same design. Wide windows let in plenty of fresh air and sunshine, a must for the health-conscious aficionados of the Arts and Crafts lifestyle.*

ABOVE: *These windows, composed of leaded clear and stained glass, bring light into an otherwise closed space. Many designers of Prairie-style windows borrowed heavily from Native American motifs, which showed an ordered geometry that managed to retain an organic feeling.*

OPPOSITE: *A central hanging stained-glass lighting fixture, created using five small individual lamps and shades, matches the sconces that light the walls. The dining room of this house—the Riordan House—holds a custom-made teardrop-shaped table that was specially designed to fit the oval space. A mirror above the built-in sideboard reflects light admirably, while stained-glass windows around the upper perimeter of the room transform entering sunlight into gold.*

RIGHT: *The ceiling light in the living room of the Heurtley House is a mesmerizing mix of geometric forms. The lights glow with the color of the sun, a theme subtly echoed below in the sunburst design of the fireplace.*

OPPOSITE: *This reproduction Roycroft chandelier in firefly-colored stained glass draws the eye upward to the ceiling's incredible beam construction. Returning to earth, the gaze falls on matching sconces, delicately arched windows, a cozy fireplace, classic Arts and Crafts furniture, and tribal rugs.*

CHAPTER FOUR
HOME FURNISHINGS

Arts and Crafts furniture is both handsome and sturdy; pieces are of versatile design, and look beautiful in combination with many other decorating styles. When heavy Mission-style furniture dominates the room, a delicate balance of wicker or twig pieces adds diversity and lightness. Antiques are still available and you may be lucky enough to come across an affordable original piece, especially if you choose generic (as opposed to signed) pieces. Generally, pieces signed with the Stickley mark, with the Roycroft orb, or by Charles Limbert are very high-priced; original pieces designed by William Morris, Charles Rennie Mackintosh, Frank Lloyd Wright, or the Greene brothers are prohibitively priced for the average budget. But don't stop visiting museum houses and galleries furnished with the creations of these masters just because you're unlikely to ever afford one; studying these justly admired designs is the best way to educate your eye and refine your tastes.

Authorized reproductions of Stickley, Roycroft, and Mackintosh furniture are available, but are, like the originals were in their own day, somewhat pricey. If you do decide to invest, be assured that these authorized reproductions are of the highest quality and that the designs are true to the originals. Many antique collectors fill in with these pieces, and they are the heirlooms of tomorrow. Some manufacturing companies have adapted various designs of Mission furniture, and offer these "reproductions" at very affordable prices. Some are of better quality and more refined style than others: careful inspection can determine the best.

A settle—what we would now call a couch—in the Arts and Crafts style and a Morris chair or rocker, complemented by small wicker tables or oak taborets (small, portable stands or tables), create a cozy yet dignified atmosphere in the living room. Coffee tables were not in use during the Arts and Crafts era, but are made today in the Mission style. A traditional, tuxedo-style sofa clad in an Arts and Crafts fabric is a great choice because it offers both comfort and great looks.

The walls of Arts and Crafts rooms can be aptly decorated using Morris-style paper or paint and stencils. Oriental rugs, dhurries, or rugs in Native American designs are appropriate atop hardwood floors or layered over a Berber broadloom rug in a natural color.

OPPOSITE: *A comfortable reclining Morris chair sits beside a rustic log and stucco fireplace in a northern Arizona log lodge. The built-in bookcase and mantel are even with the molding that circles the room. In traditional Arts and Crafts style, an appliquéd linen portiere subtly divides rooms and diverts drafts.*

Simple window treatments such as stenciled or embroidered curtains, rather than drapes, are the most appropriate. Venetian blinds or roll-down bamboo or matchstick blinds are all in keeping with the Arts and Crafts style; they offer privacy and keep the handsome woodwork of window frames visible.

Textiles such as table linens and pillow covers add needed pattern and color to the Arts and Crafts room. Runners on dining room tables and buffets and dresser scarves in bedrooms may also be stenciled or embroidered; stylized nature motifs were and are by far the most popular. Pillows on chairs and settles add comfort and color.

The various approaches to furnishing kitchens and bathrooms alone could provide enough material for an entire chapter, but we will touch here only on the basics. Because a decorated kitchen and an indoor bathroom were new ideas at the turn of the century, most of the furnishings were some shade of white or gray, perhaps with a touch of black or dark green. This color scheme can still make an attractive and authentic look, but wood in the bathroom or kitchen is also appropriate and offers a more elegant, updated option. Glass-paned cabinets are available today in the Craftsman style. Original and reproduction bathroom fixtures sport brass or chrome hardware, and Arts and Crafts–style lighting to match is also available. When it comes to these two

functional and important rooms, look for a blend of state-of-the-art luxury and historical inspiration, and buy the best you can afford.

The sparse design of Arts and Crafts–style rooms often seen in books and magazines can seem impossible to achieve to clutter-bound enthusiasts. A separate room to hold all the family's things just isn't available to most of us. The Arts and Crafts lifestyle is a call to simplify, but remember to be realistic. If you tend to accumulate lots of things, opt for the warmer-looking rooms that incorporate pottery and paintings, baskets and magazines. If, on the other hand, you're something of a minimalist, the sparer style may suit.

Pulling all the elements of the Arts and Crafts home together—the spindled and slatted furniture mixed with wicker pieces; the warm glow of period lighting; and colorful textiles, carpets, stencils, and wallpapers—is an art in itself. Decorative details, such as art pottery and decorative metal objects, paintings, woodblock prints, and period books and magazines are the adhesive that helps to hold the design scheme together.

The Arts and Crafts style is inviting and unpretentious, and yet, in its simplicity, it is very sophisticated. It has both honesty and integrity. Family and guests are sure to feel "at home" in the Arts and Crafts rooms you create.

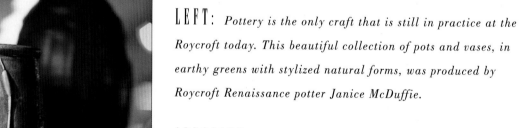

LEFT: *Pottery is the only craft that is still in practice at the Roycroft today. This beautiful collection of pots and vases, in earthy greens with stylized natural forms, was produced by Roycroft Renaissance potter Janice McDuffie.*

OPPOSITE: *A simple sturdy rocking chair is the centerpiece of this Arts and Crafts tableau. The Prairie-style house is infused with warm gold color, due to the combined effect of the windows, wood, and paint. Handsome textiles and an art pottery vase filled with branches add stylized accents of nature.*

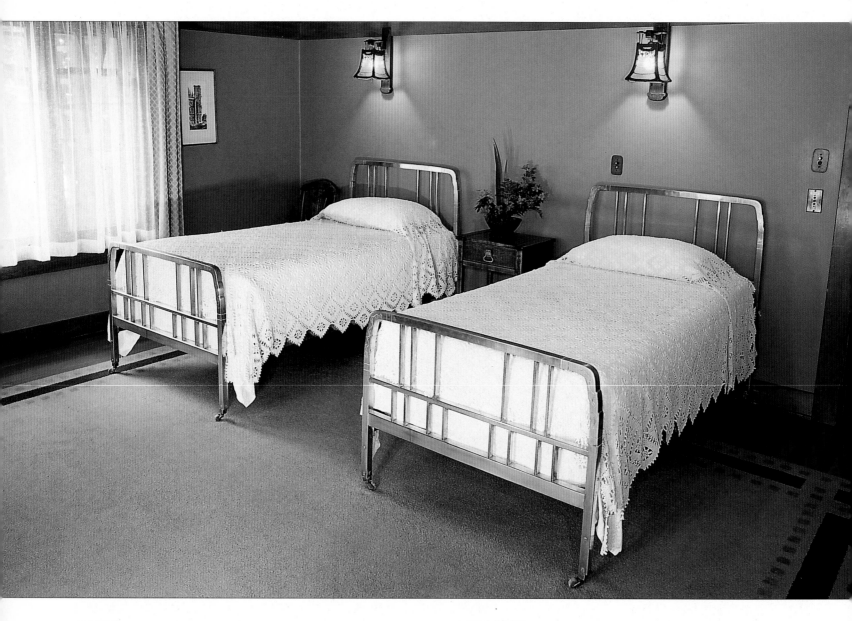

ABOVE: *These rare polished nickel beds stand in the guest room of the Gamble House. The architects, Greene & Greene, designed both the furniture and the lighting sconces. Silvergray walls and carpeting are lightened further by sheer curtains and white lace bedspreads. Roll-down shades, which have been built into the space above the windows, provide privacy for this first-floor bedroom.*

OPPOSITE: *Strong wood trim, diamond-pane windows dressed with sheer curtains, and a Craftsman lantern combine to make this cottage bedroom romantic and cozy.*

OPPOSITE: *A sleeping porch built adjacent to a bedroom/sitting room is typical of Arts and Crafts styling. The window and French door between the two rooms allow light and air to filter through to the windowless inner room.*

ABOVE: *A reproduction spindled Stickley dining room set recalls the simple, elegant designs of craftsman Harvey Ellis. Artwork and accessories give the room a lift and add color to balance the heavy wood.*

LEFT, TOP: *Select Arts and Crafts touches mix with pieces in a range of other styles to create a comfortable reading and writing corner. The barrel chair in an early Frank Lloyd Wright design pulls up to a generic desk. A mica-shaded floor lamp bathes the modern upholstered chair and ottoman with soft light. Family photographs straddle the eras, and French doors open to an outdoor sitting area.*

LEFT, BOTTOM: *Arts and Crafts kitchens are often adapted by 1990s families to include twentieth-century convenience and the best of nineteenth-century design. Generally, the kitchen had lighter wood and wall colors than other rooms in the house, and this look translates well for today. This modern kitchen in an old house is ideal—its slate floor and generous lighting are functional and beautiful.*

OPPOSITE: *The masculine look of this console table and dark wooden wainscot are softened by old-fashioned wisteria in a pottery vase. The gently curving wall sconces and the Japanese triptych above the table balance the severity of the tile floor.*

RIGHT, TOP: *Every Arts and Crafts element is included in this living room made up entirely of reproduction pieces. Period colors and patterns are found in the stenciled frieze, upholstery, and carpet; stained and leaded glass separate the room from its adjoining space; and books and a copper and mica lamp accessorize the room. The spindled cube chair and settle are lighter in color and scale than most Mission pieces.*

RIGHT, BOTTOM: *Open French doors make a dining room and living room one space for entertaining, but can be closed after dinner. The minstrel's balcony, which was originally designed to be used by musicians who provided entertainment during parties, is a gracious feature, but also offers a cozy place to read or write.*

OPPOSITE: *Arts and Crafts textiles and a mica-shaded lamp punctuate this traditional bedroom in a modern suburban house. The art pottery vase and pedestal reinforce the subtle Arts and Crafts styling.*

ABOVE: *This distinctive china, originally designed for the Roycroft Inn circa 1905, sports a stylized Native American motif. The pieces bear the Roycroft insignia and are as durable as commercial hotelware.*

RIGHT: *A dining room in a new home is furnished with reproduction Arts and Crafts furniture and handmade linens decorated with the stylized natural designs of the period. Crossing runners were popular in part because they allow the fine wood and superior construction of the table to remain visible. Arts and Crafts paintings, clocks, candlesticks, and curtains accessorize the room and compensate for a space that lacks the architectural details and lovely wood trim present in a period house.*

RIGHT, TOP:

Freestanding kitchen furniture and built-in counters and cabinets are all appropriate in the Arts and Crafts kitchen. Here, the upper cabinets have glass fronts and geometric mullions. Note the pass-through counter that, with the lift of a wooden divider, spans both the kitchen and the pantry.

RIGHT, BOTTOM:

An array of textiles— from striped and plaid wool blankets to a Native American print used as upholstery to a stylized floral on the chair cushion— add pattern and color to this Arts and Crafts room. Note the very simple window curtains, which complement rather than clash.

OPPOSITE: *The focus of this cozy room is its massive cut-stone fireplace, which is surrounded by period Arts and Crafts furnishings. The couch and chairs have been updated with new Morris-designed fabrics where leather would originally have been.*

LEFT: *This large bathroom has all the modern conveniences but retains a period look. The abundance of oak, together with a tile floor, metal hardware on the cabinets, and Arts and Crafts–style wall lanterns, imbue the room with its Craftsman flair. Even the details— from the wicker-wrapped toothbrush holder to the turquoise pottery to the period wall colors visible in the mirror—are in keeping with the Arts and Crafts styling.*

ABOVE: *The Roycroft cabinet is made for books, but could hold any collection or a TV. Note the carved Roycroft orb, emblazoned on the front door as both a decorative feature and a proclamation of the fine quality of Roycroft furniture. Metal hardware adds to the distinctiveness of the piece.*

RIGHT: *The master bedroom in Frank Lloyd Wright's own home features a massive Prairie-style bed and dresser designed by the architect himself. A mural above the door and a repeating pattern along the room's frieze are lit by hanging pendant lamps. The vaulted beamed ceiling—somewhat unusual in a bedroom—is simply awe-inspiring.*

LEFT: *A rare Charles Rohlfs chair complements beautifully the Stickley spindle settle and small oak taboret in this Arts and Crafts living room. Plump pillows, one embroidered in a popular Arts and Crafts design, decorate the settle and make its wooden back more comfortable. A lamp shaded with amber glass and a handmade Persian rug add additional color and warmth; the plein air painting invokes the spirit of nature.*

RIGHT: *This elegant bathroom boasts an unusual sunken, tiled, L-shaped tub. Colors are muted to promote relaxation in the bath. A marble sink surround and Prairie-style leaded-glass window and French door are an integral part of the pared-down but sophisticated look.*

LEFT: *Only Frank Lloyd Wright could achieve this spectacular space. The drama of its arched ceiling is a strict counterpoint to the squared masses of simple furniture. Balances such as these are essential to successful Arts and Crafts design.*

LEFT: *A cabinet designed by Charles Limbert is a spectacular focus for this space. Softened by the graceful arch of the apron and by glass windows, this piece is a true collector's item.*

OPPOSITE: *A super-modern background works wonderfully with this Prairie-style furniture. The spare look is exciting and relaxing by turns.*

ABOVE: *Both the setting and the furniture in the dining room of the D.M. Francis House are premium Arts and Crafts. This handsome table and chairs are original Roycroft. The table is topped with stenciled and hemstitched crossing runners and is well laid with Roycroft Renaissance china. A fireplace, built-in sideboard, and French doors opening onto a sunroom complete the authenticity of the room.*

RIGHT: *A collection of high-back dining chairs grouped around the table creates a room within a room, an idea first conceived by Arts and Crafts architects. Note the lamp at each corner of the table; this is a feature unique to Frank Lloyd Wright houses. This dining room in the Meyer-May House also features a painted mural framed by horizontal ceiling moldings. The furniture, carpet, and lighting were all designed by Wright.*

ABOVE: *Fireplace mantels have always made desirable shelves. Here, a wooden mantel set against a stone chimney houses a collection of pottery and hammered copper pieces.*

OPPOSITE: *Built-in lighted bookcases occupy either side of the stone fireplace in this charming room. Navajo rugs and Native American artifacts are very appropriate Arts and Crafts accents.*

RIGHT: *This Arts and Crafts master bedroom is a careful mix of old and new. Reproduction furniture, mica and stained-glass lamps, original plein-air paintings in period frames, and appropriate new textiles coordinate in a setting that captures the essence of Arts and Crafts style. A beamed ceiling and a wall of French windows and doors make this space airy and authentic.*

LEFT: *Frank Lloyd Wright's own dining room in Oak Park, Illinois, is adorned with a sky light behind a decorative grille instead of the more traditional chandelier. Windows at standing height let in additional natural light while ensuring privacy.*

OPPOSITE: *This Roycroft rocker and bureau are enriched by a wonderful dresser-top vignette. A stained-glass and silver lamp, vintage photographs, a decanter, and a brush and comb set are artfully arranged atop a white dresser scarf. Sheer curtains further brighten the corner of this Arts and Crafts bedroom.*